Meet the Shapes™ Coloring Book

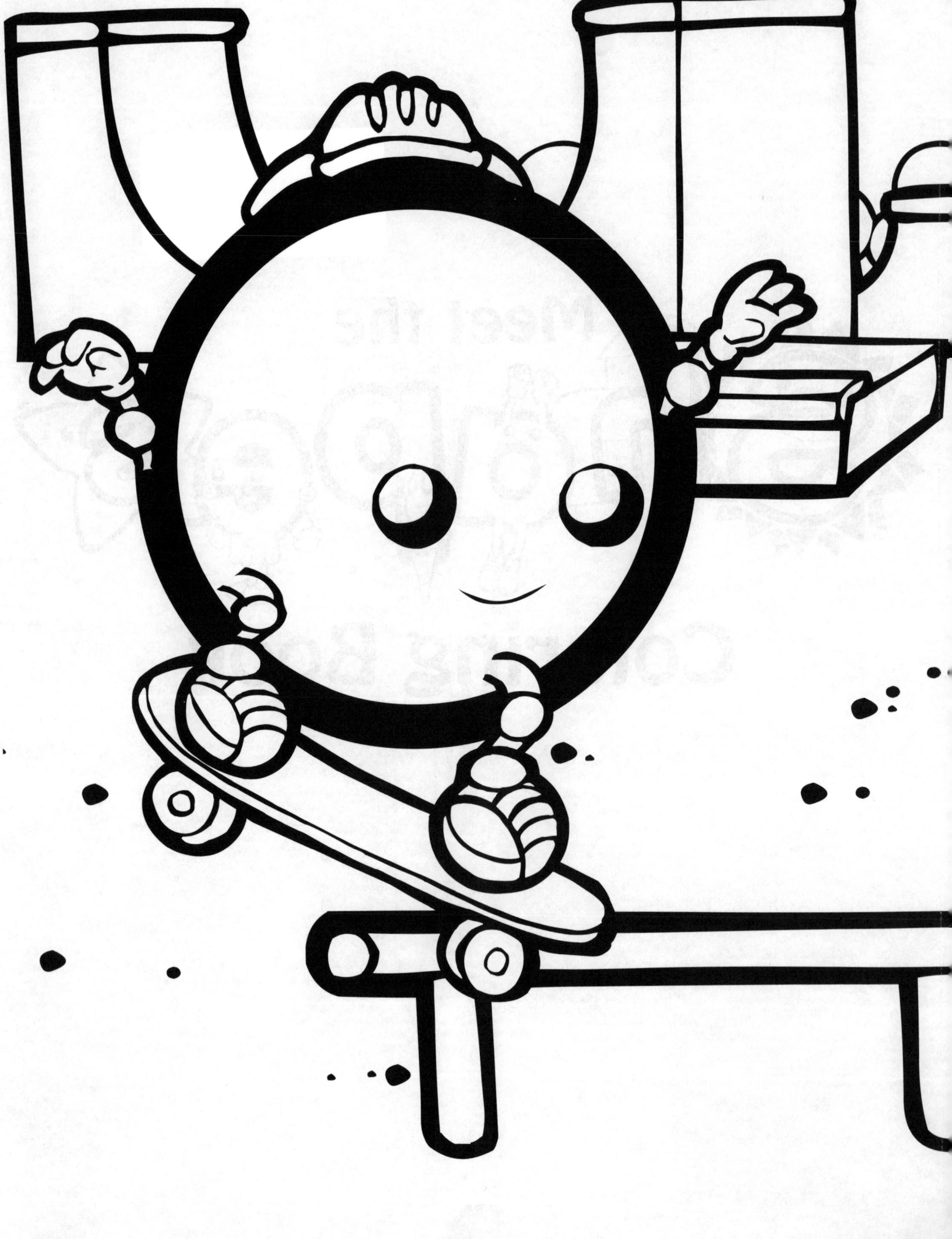

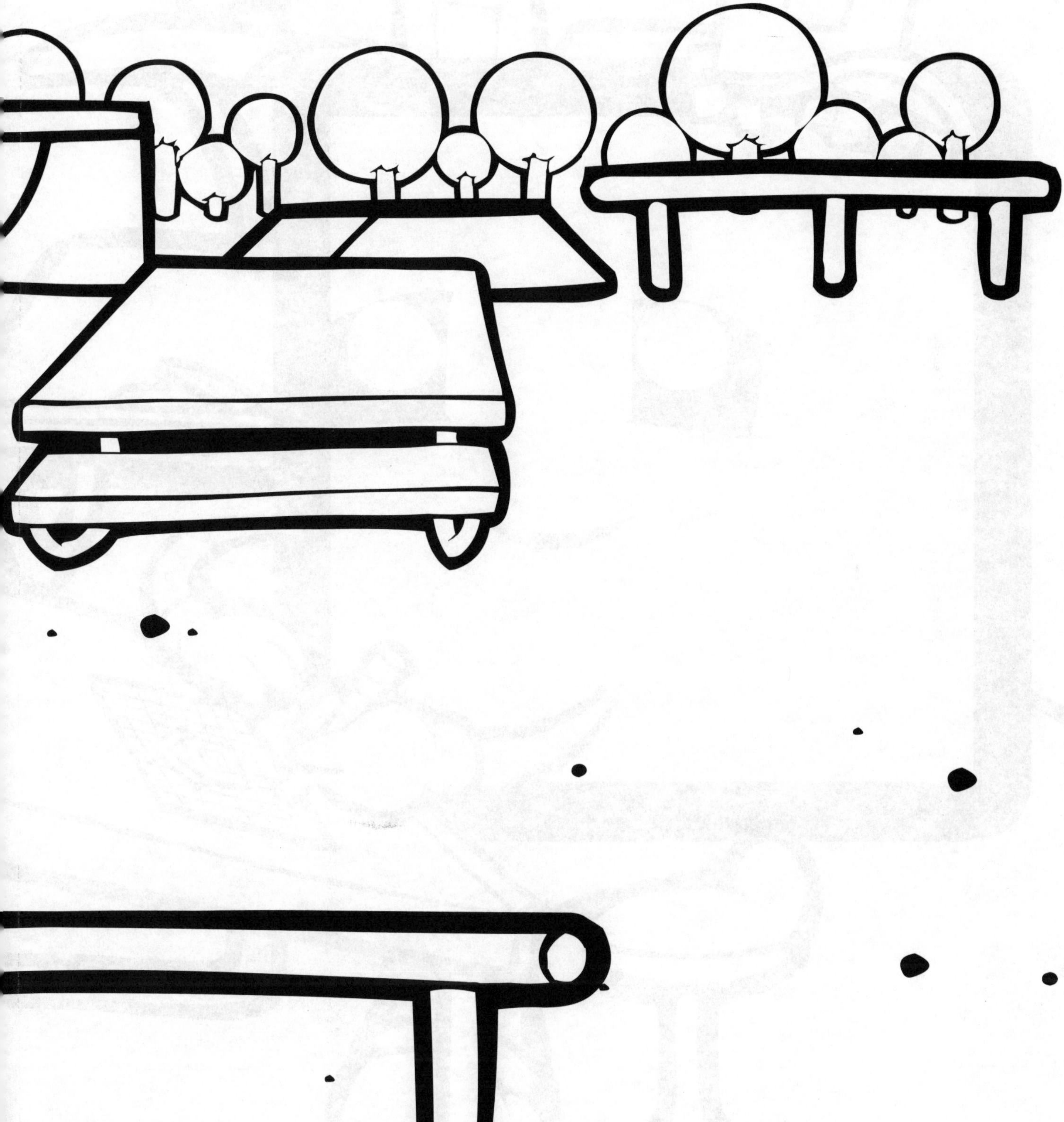

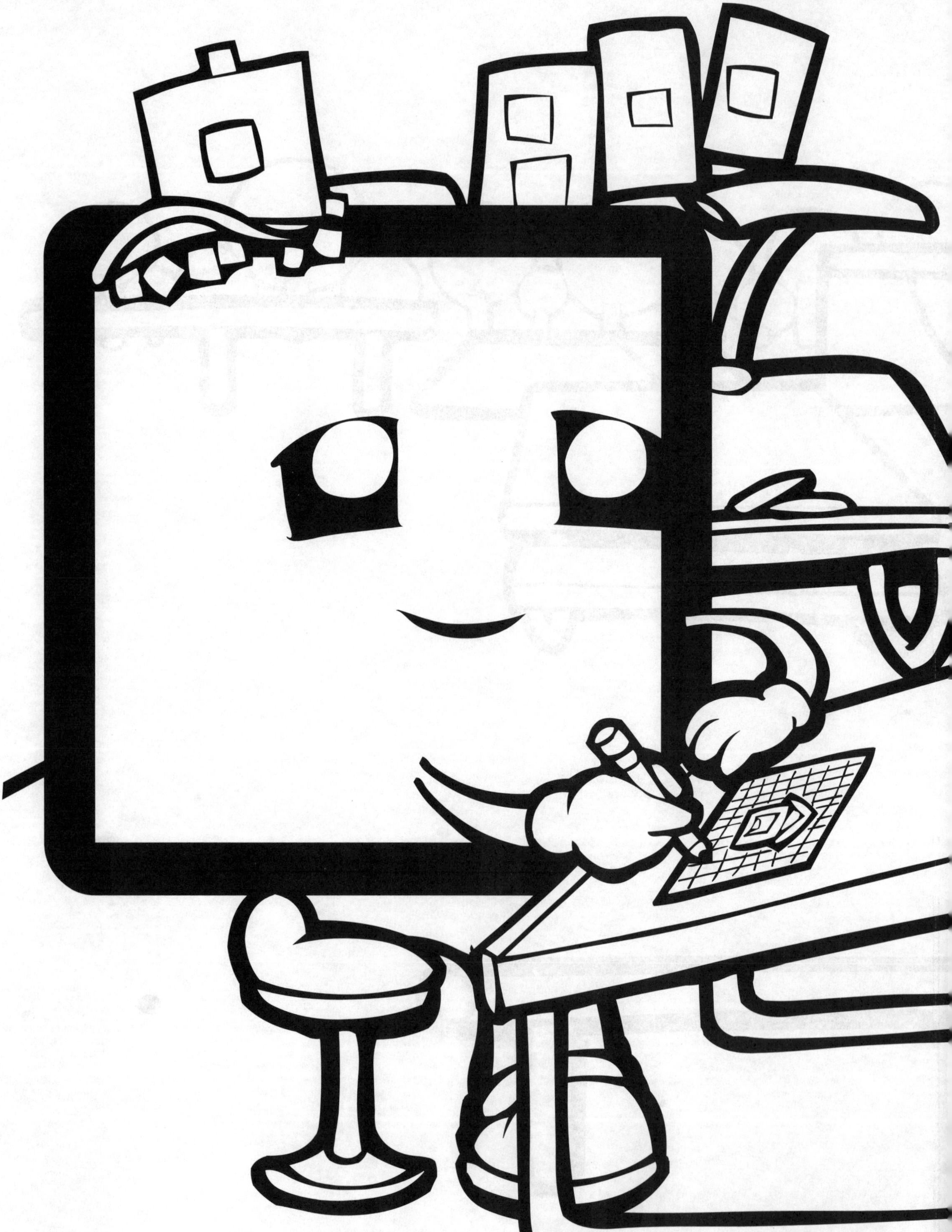

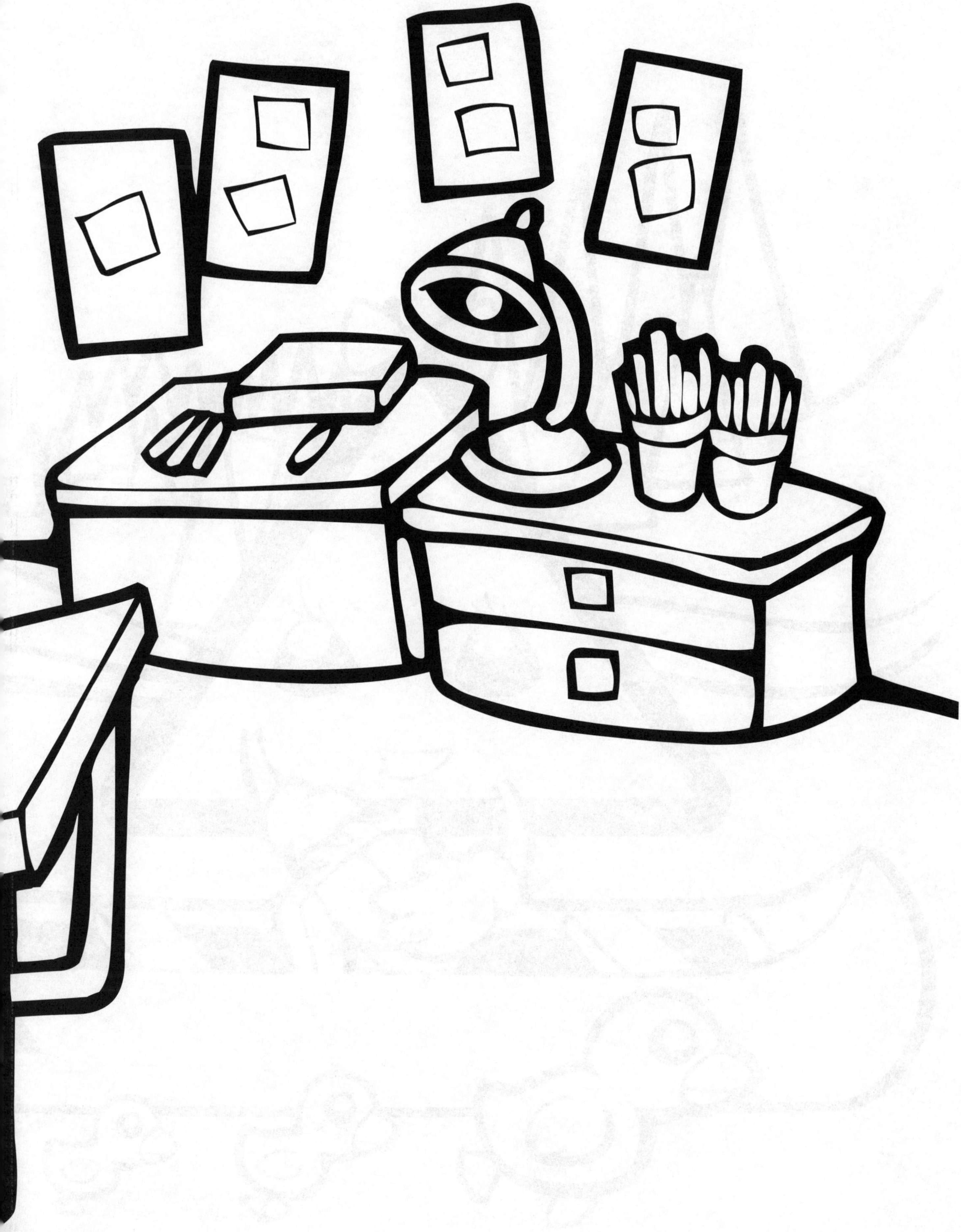

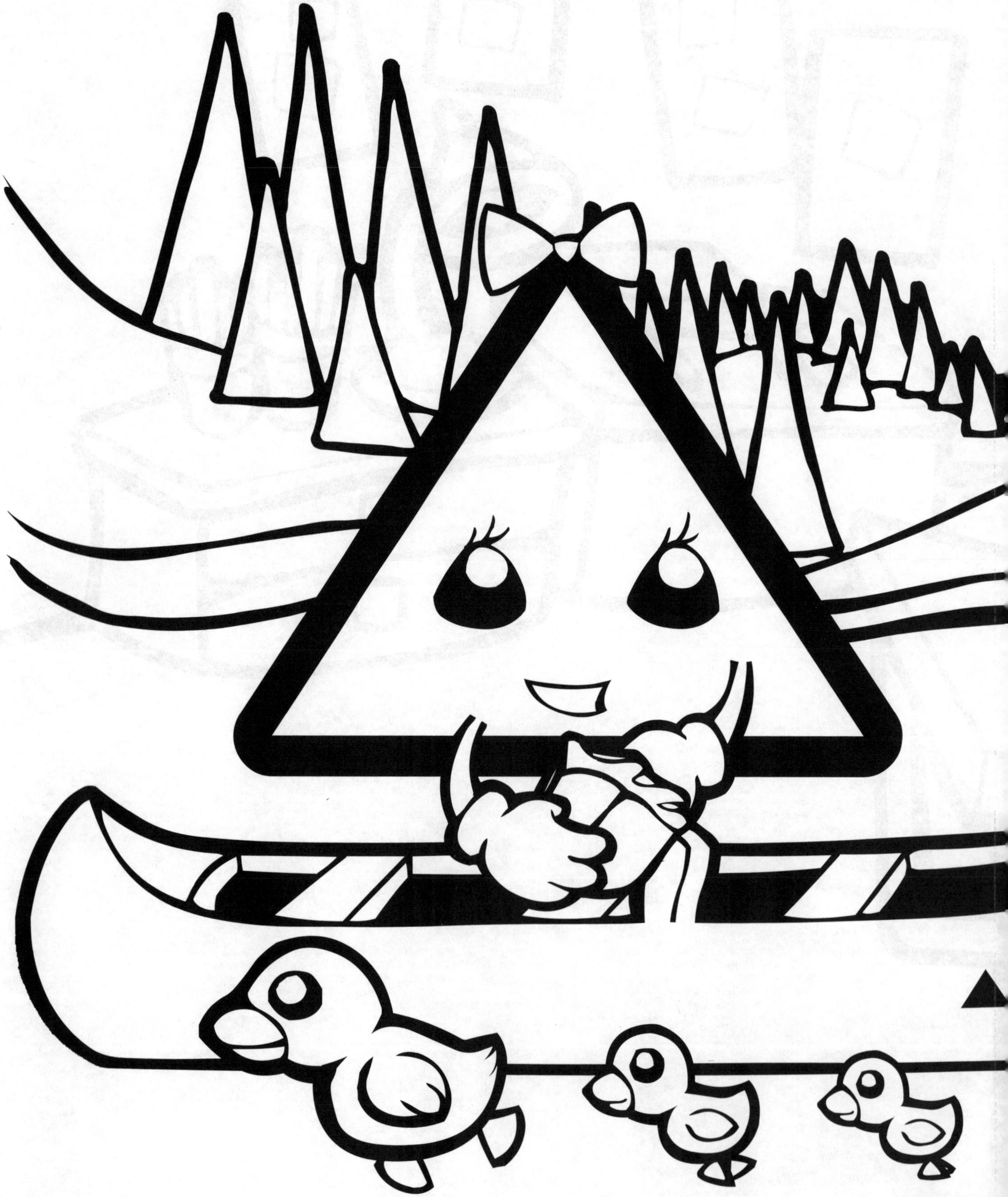

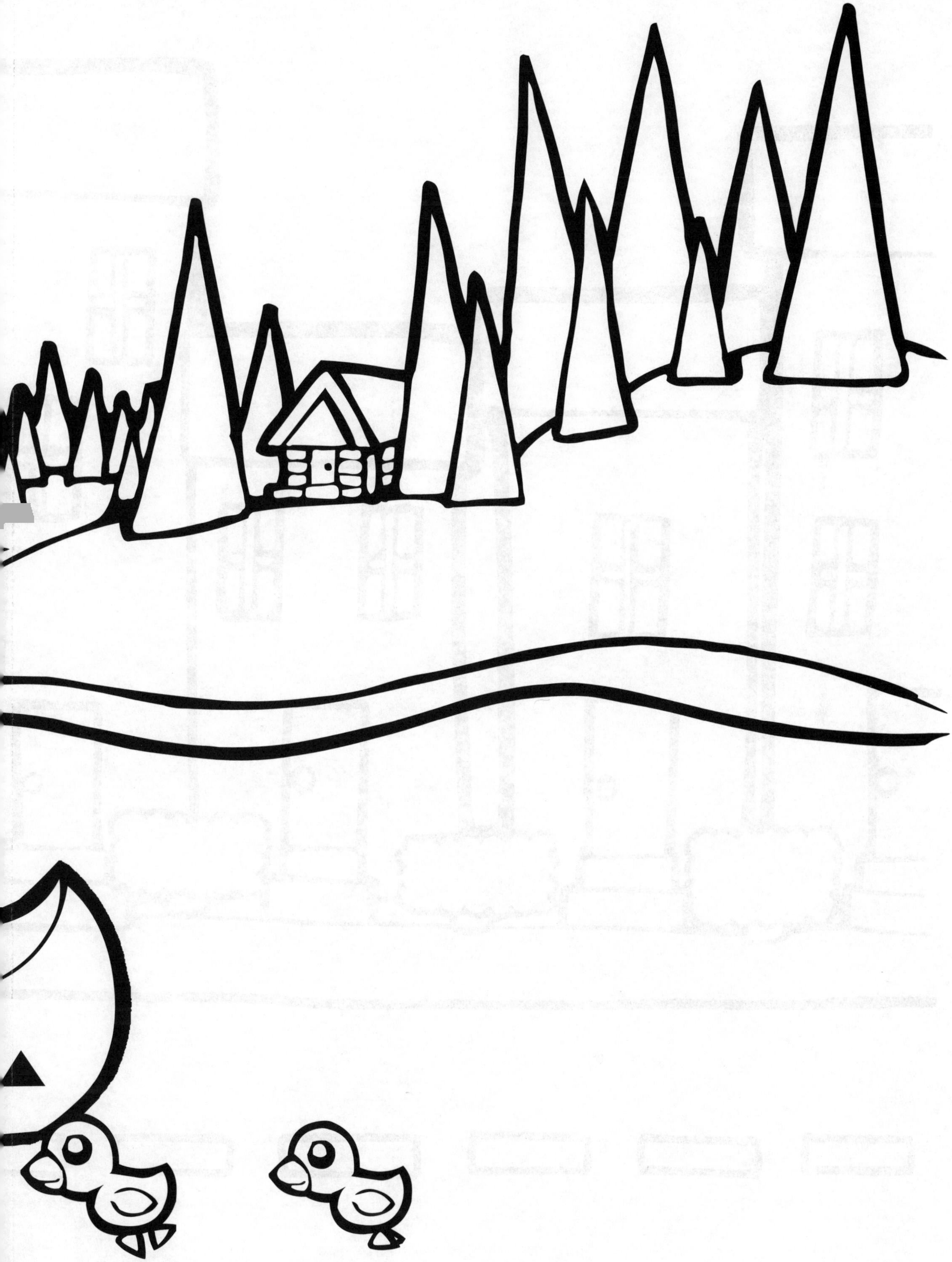

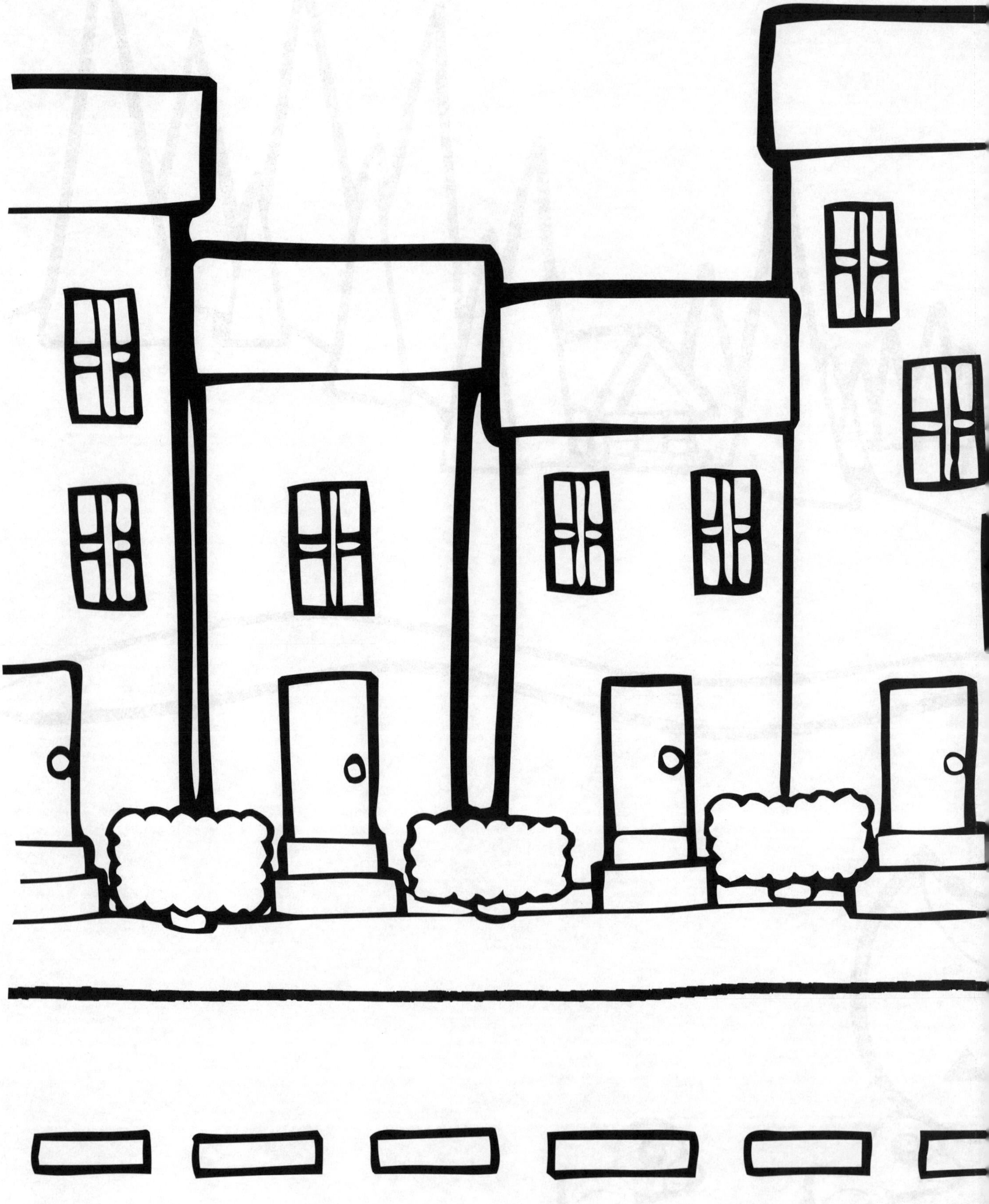

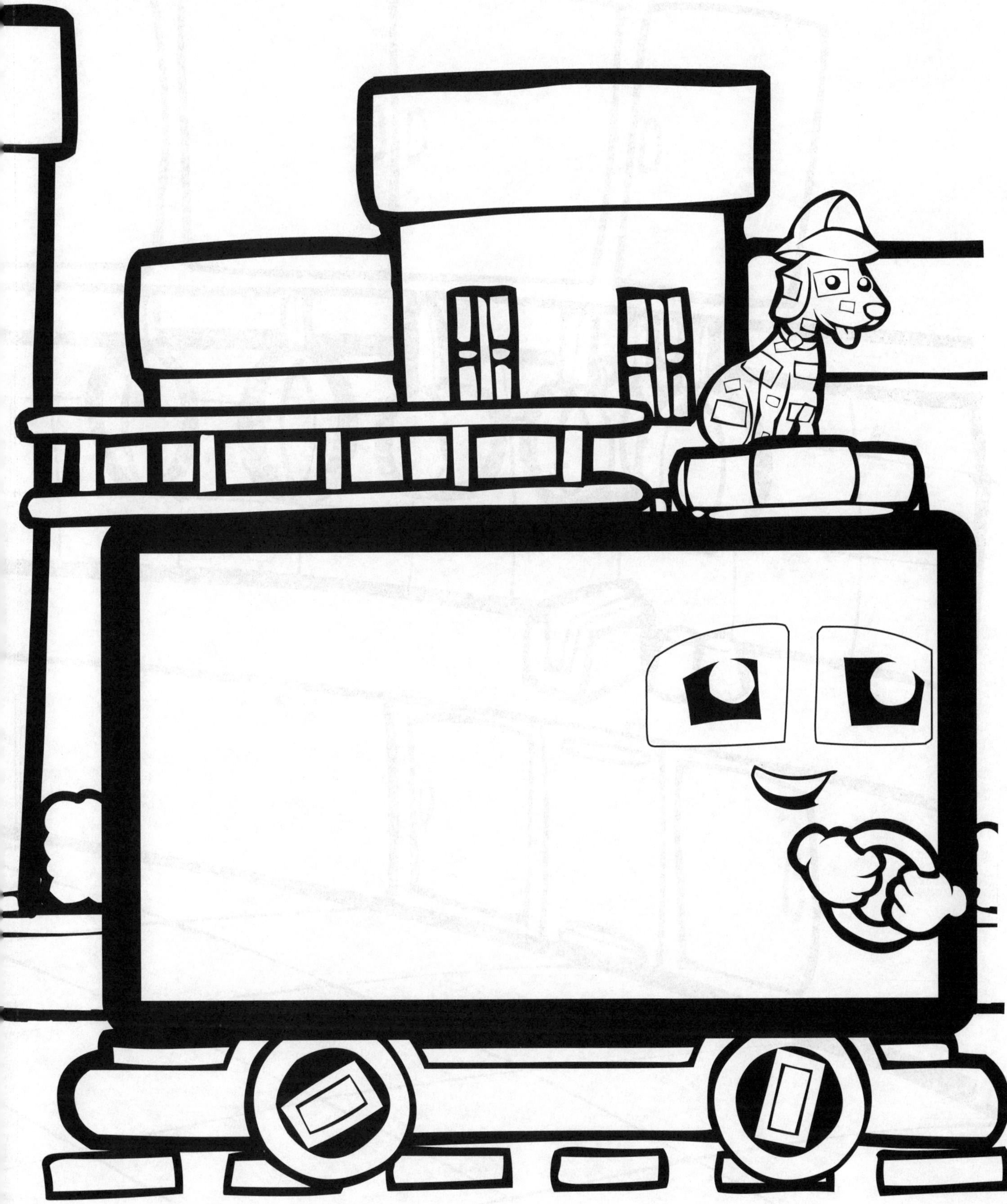

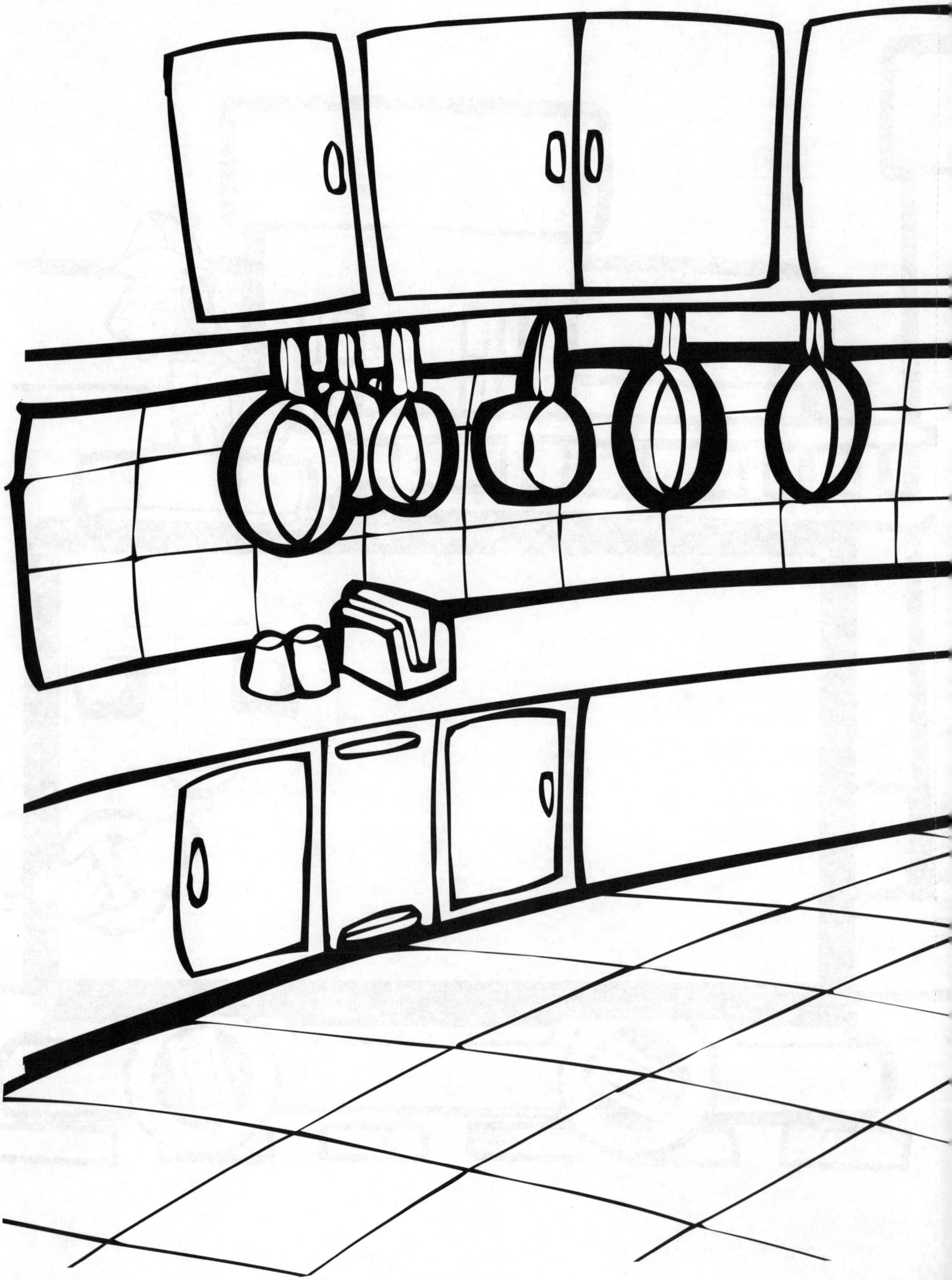

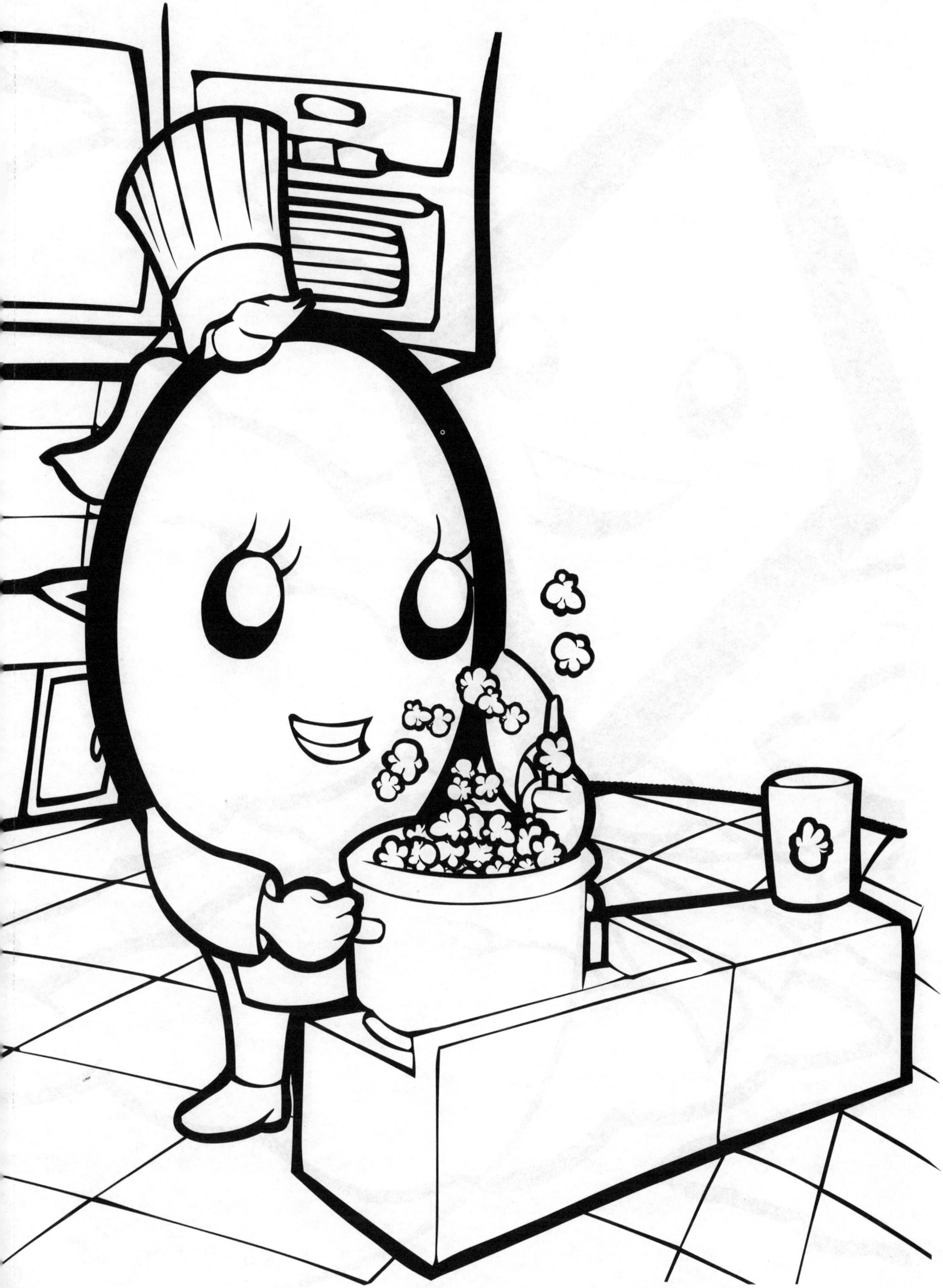

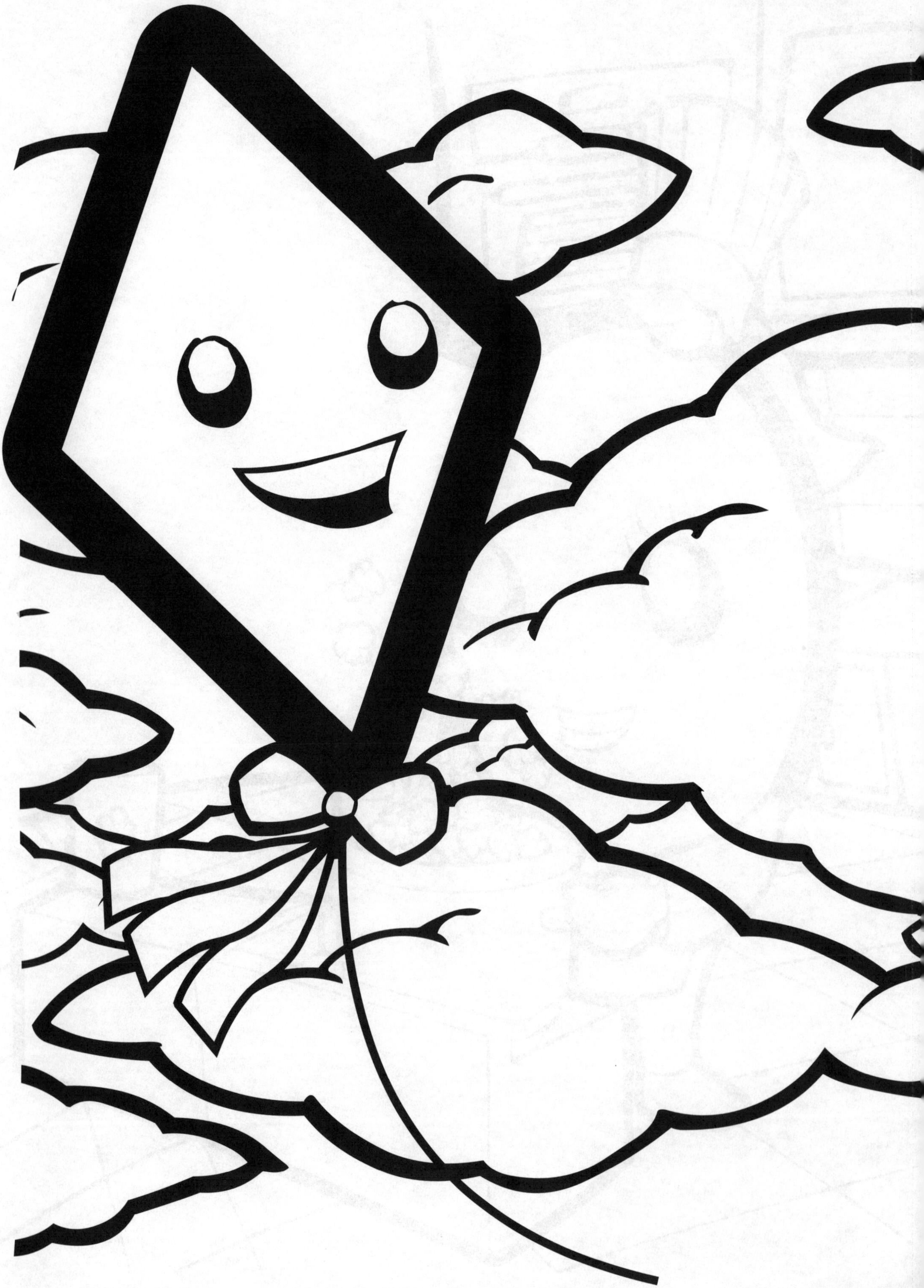

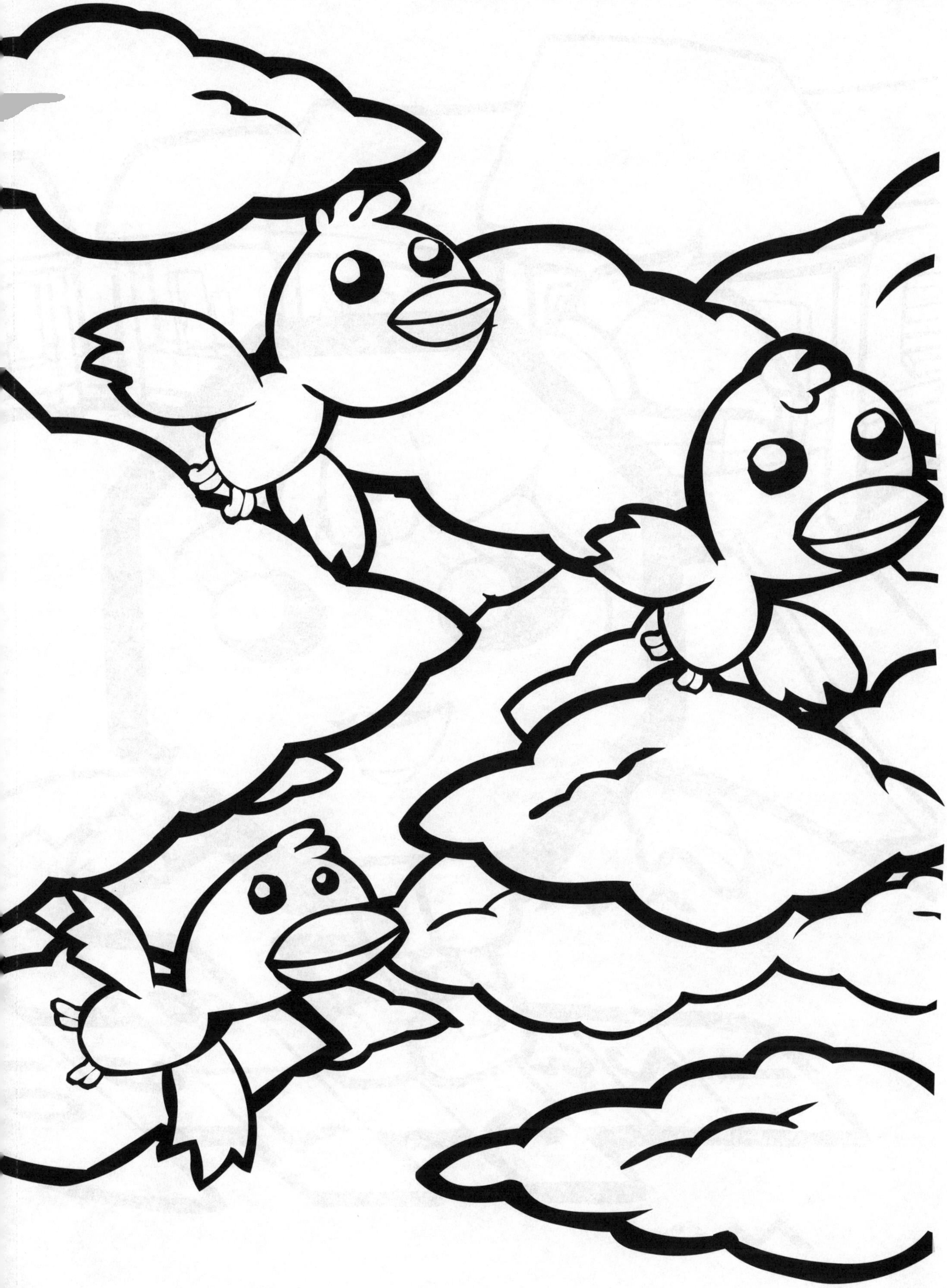

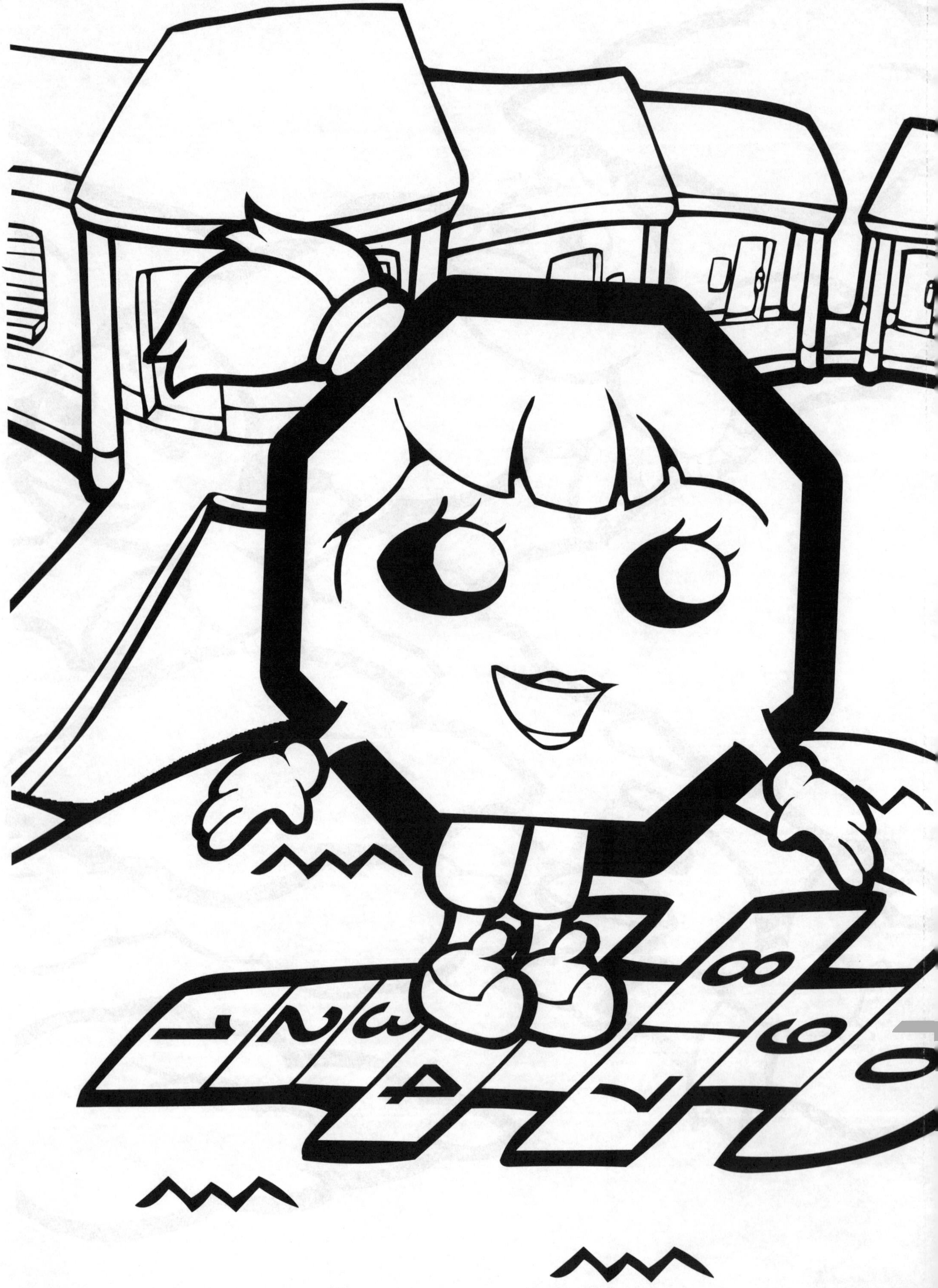

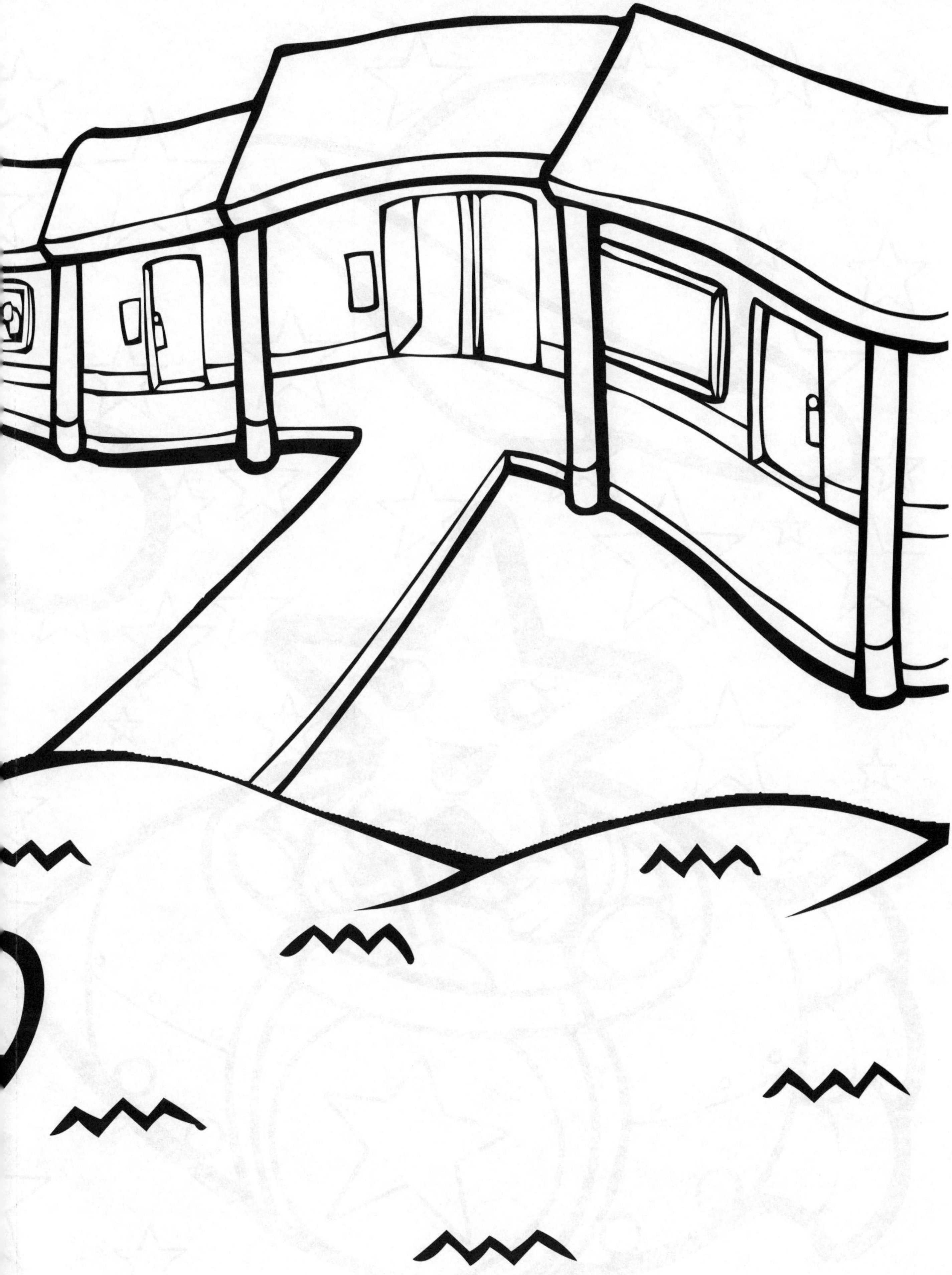

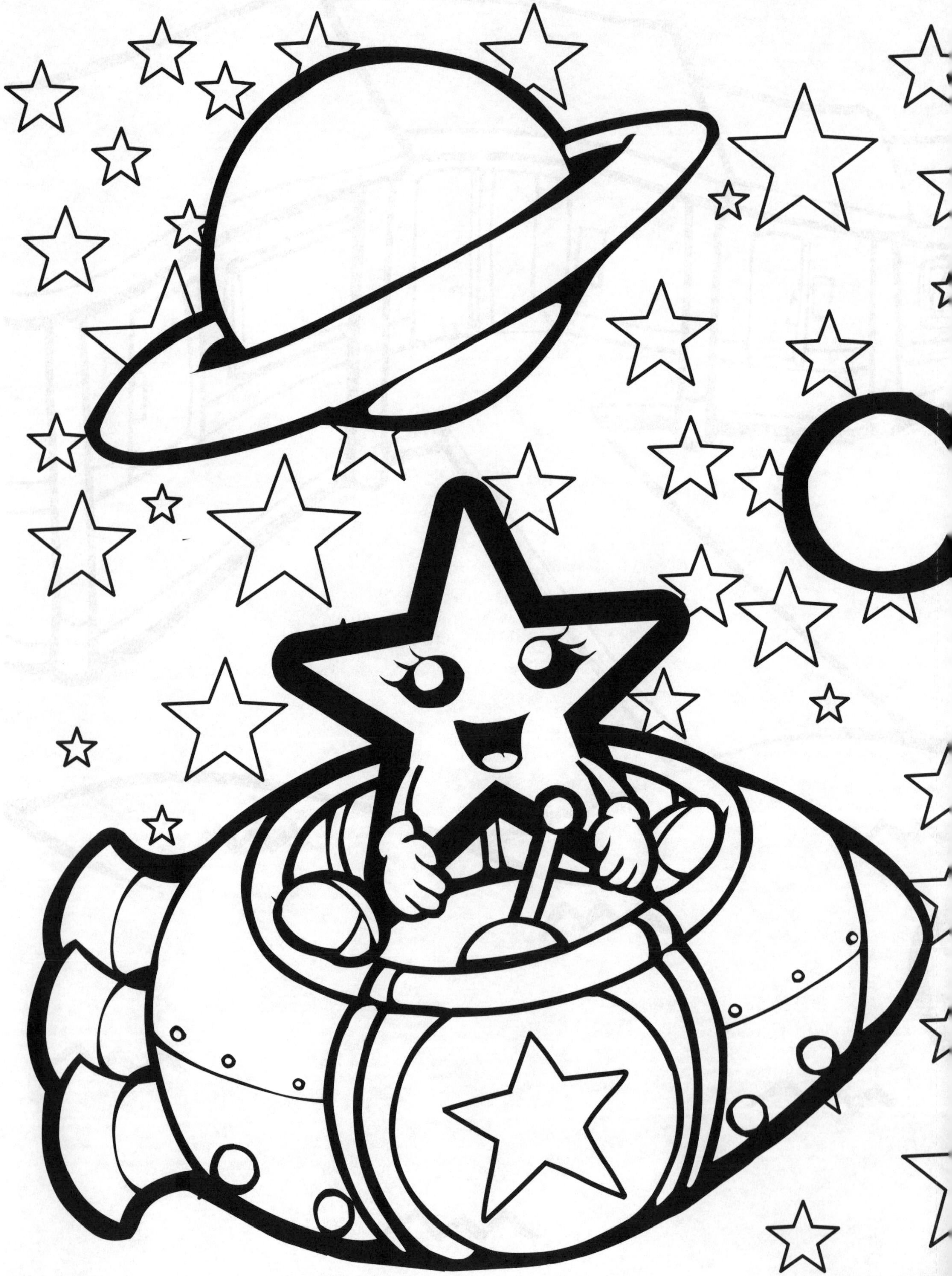

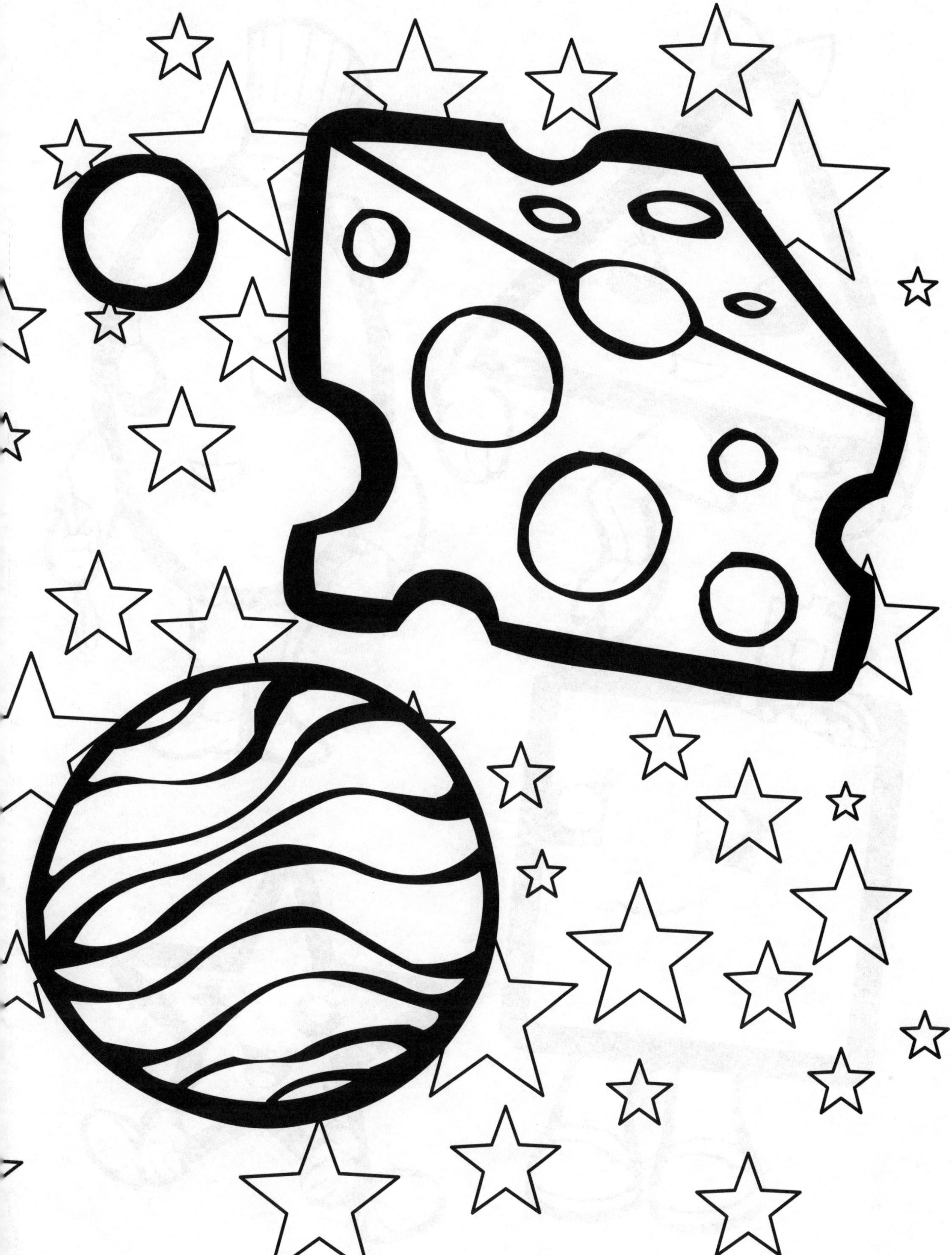

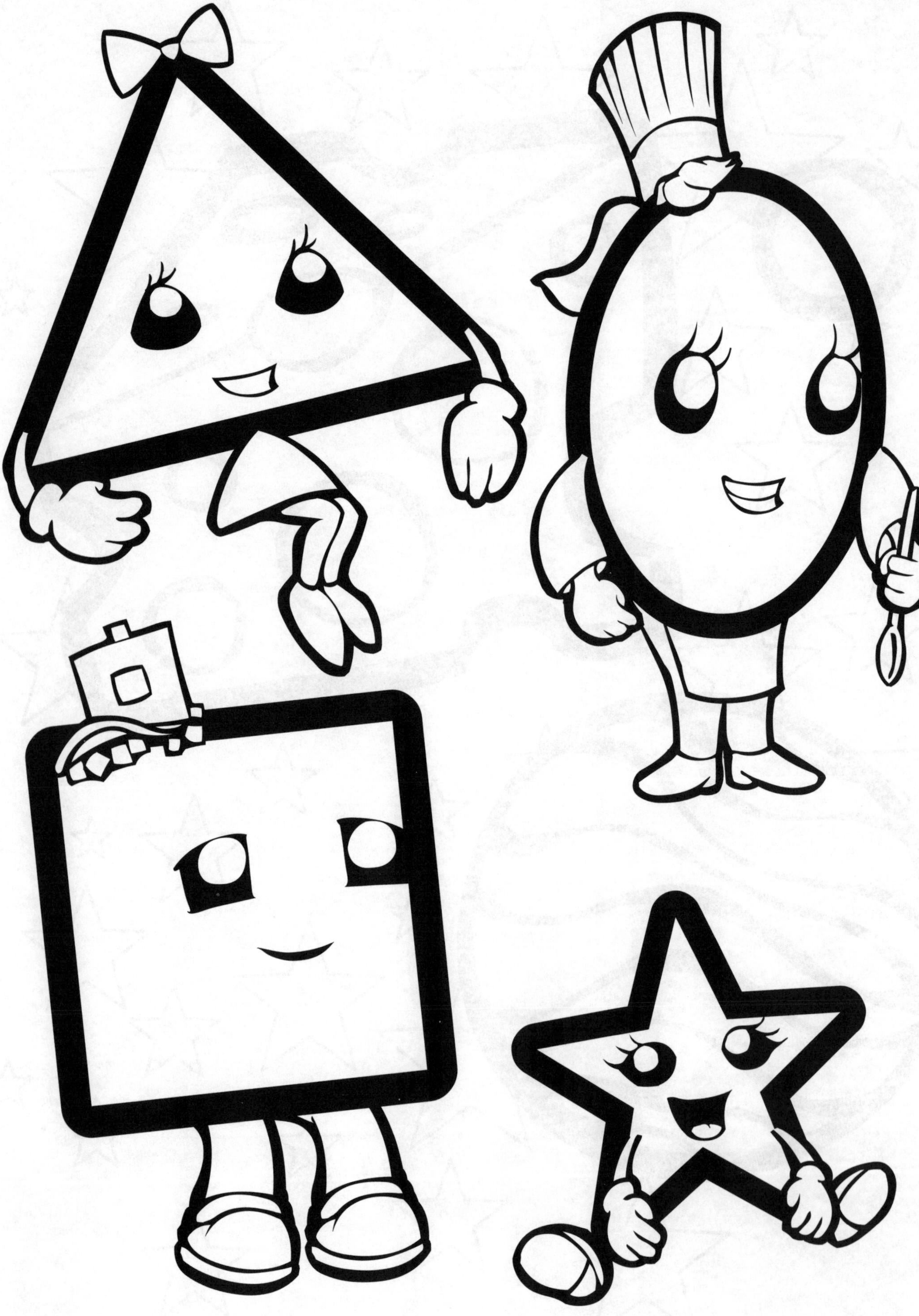

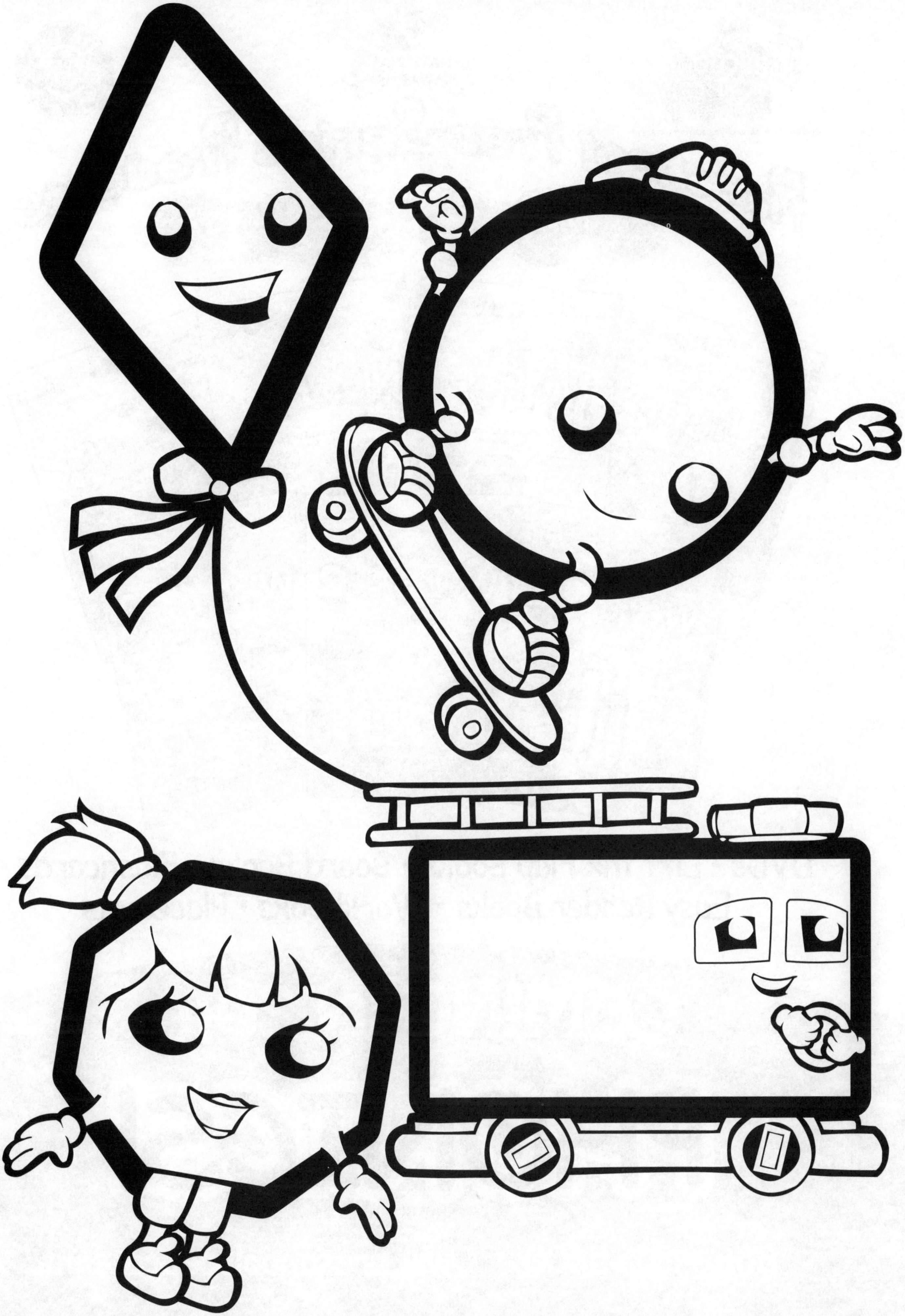